*E*verything worthwhile was done
By small steps taken one by one.

— J. D. Freeman

Other Bestselling
Blue Mountain Arts®
Books

By Susan Polis Schutz:
To My Daughter, with Love, on the Important Things in Life
To My Son with Love
I Love You

100 Things to Always Remember... and One Thing to Never Forget
by Alin Austin

Is It Time to Make a Change?
by Deanna Beisser

Trust in Yourself
by Donna Fargo

To the One Person I Consider to Be My Soul Mate
by D. Pagels

For You, Just Because You're Very Special to Me
by Collin McCarty

Chasing Away the Clouds
by Douglas Pagels

Anthologies:
42 Gifts I'd Like to Give to You
Always Believe in Yourself and Your Dreams
Creeds of Life, Love, & Inspiration
For You, My Daughter
Friends Are Forever
Friends for Life
I Love You, Mom
I'm Glad You Are My Sister
The Joys and Challenges of Motherhood
Life Can Be Hard Sometimes ...but It's Going to Be Okay
Marriage Is a Promise of Love
Mottos to Live By
Take Each Day One Step at a Time
Teaching and Learning Are Lifelong Journeys
There Is Greatness Within You, My Son
These Are the Gifts I'd Like to Give to You
Think Positive Thoughts Every Day
Thoughts of Friendship
Thoughts to Share with a Wonderful Teenager
To My Child
True Friends Always Remain in Each Other's Heart
With God by Your Side ...You Never Have to Be Alone
Words of Love
You're Just like a Sister to Me

The Language
of
Recovery
...and Living Life
One Day at a Time

*A Blue Mountain Arts®
Collection*

Blue Mountain Press®

SPS Studios, Inc., Boulder, Colorado

Library of Congress Catalog Card Number: 00-035244
ISBN: 0-88396-561-5

ACKNOWLEDGMENTS appear on page 64.

Poems by Susan Polis Schutz appearing in this publication: Copyright © 1979 Continental Publications; © 1989 Stephen Schutz and Susan Polis Schutz.

 Registered in the U.S. Patent and Trademark Office.
Certain trademarks are used under license.

Manufactured in the United States of America
First Printing: July 2000

This book is printed on recycled paper.

Library of Congress Cataloging-in-Publication Data

The language of recovery : —and living life one day at a time : a Blue Mountain Arts collection.—[Enl. ed.]
        p. cm.
    ISBN 0-88396-561-5 (pbk. : alk. paper)
    1. Conduct of life—Quotations, maxims, etc. 2. Conduct of life—Poetry. I. SPS Studios.

 PN6084.C556 L36   2000b
 082—dc21

                                                                                    00-035244

SPS Studios, Inc.
P.O. Box 4549, Boulder, Colorado 80306

Contents

(Authors listed in order of first appearance)

The Path
to Recovery

Nobody ever said that it would be easy, or that the skies would always be sunny. When gray days and worrisome times come along, you need to stay strong. Know that everything will be okay.

When life has got you down, remember: it's <u>okay</u> to feel vulnerable. You feel things deeply, and that is a wonderful quality to have. Rest assured that, in the long run, the good days will <u>far</u> outnumber the bad.

What is sometimes perceived as weakness is actually strength. The more you're bothered by something that's wrong, the more you're empowered to make things right. Each day is like a room you spend time in before you move on to the next. And in each room — filled with possibilities — there is a door that leads to more serenity in life.

Leave behind any little worries. Tomorrow they won't matter, and next month you may not even remember what they were. Take the others <u>one at a time</u>, and you'll be amazed at how your difficulties manage to become easier.

Find your smile. Warm yourself with your quiet determination and your knowledge of brighter days ahead. Do the things that need to be done. Say the words that need to be said.

Happiness is waiting for you. Believe in your ability. Cross your bridges. Listen to your heart. Your faith in tomorrow will <u>always</u> help you do what is right... and it will help you be strong along the path to recovery.

— Collin McCarty

When It's Time for a New Beginning...

You need faith. That things will be better.
You need strength. And you'll find it within.
You need patience and persistence.
You need hope, and you need to keep it close
    to the center of everything that means the
    most to you.

You need to put things in perspective.
So much of your life lies ahead!
You need to know how good it can be.
You need to take the best of what you've learned
    from the old, and bring it to the beautiful days
    of a new journey.

Life's new beginnings happen for very special
reasons. When it's time to move on, remember that
it <u>really</u> is okay. Because when a new beginning
unfolds in the story of your life, you go such a
    long way toward making the dreams
    of your tomorrows come true.

— Douglas Pagels

Living Life
One Day at a Time

Our lives are made up of a million moments, spent in a million different ways. Some are spent searching for love, peace, and harmony. Others are spent surviving day to day. But there is no greater moment than when we find that life — with all its joys and sorrows — is meant to be lived one day at a time.

It's in this knowledge that we discover the most wonderful truth of all. Whether we live in a forty-room mansion, surrounded by servants and wealth, or find it a struggle to manage the rent month to month, we have it within our power to be fully satisfied and live a life with true meaning.

One day at a time — we have that ability, through cherishing each moment and rejoicing in each dream. We can experience each day anew, and with this fresh start we have what it takes to make all of our dreams come true. Each day is new, and living one day at a time enables us to truly enjoy life and live it to the fullest.

— Regina Hill

KNOW THAT THINGS WILL GET BETTER

——————— ❧ ———————

The natural healing force within each one of us is the greatest force in getting well.

— Hippocrates

Every situation, properly perceived, becomes an opportunity to heal.

— A Course in Miracles

The great thing
in this world
is not so much
where we are,
but in what direction
we are moving.

— Oliver Wendell Holmes

Sometimes, we are overwhelmed
    with the obstacles
we are given in our lives,
and we ask, "Why me?"
And often, when the answers elude us,
we believe that the trials
    through which we suffer
are unfair and harsh.
But there <u>are</u> answers, even though
    we may not recognize them.
In this world, we are all connected,
and there is a reason for whatever happens.
We must remain strong in the face of adversity
and meet the challenges one day at a time.
And as time heals us, both body and soul,
we may come to understand the meaning
    of our trials
or recognize the good that came from them.
We may take pride in knowing that we
    made it through them,
and as a result are much stronger
than we were before.
When we are going through
a difficult time in life,
we must accept what has happened
and know that things
    will get better.

— Judith Mammay

What Is Recovery?

Rebuilding our lives,
Restoring ourselves,
Picking up the pieces,
Healing from past wounds,
Regaining our hope,
Obtaining self-respect,
Mending broken spirits,
Making amends for the spirits we've broken,
Reclaiming our right to be,
Releasing what doesn't belong to us,
Raising up what does without fear,
Repossessing our minds and our hearts,
Repairing broken thoughts and faulty behaviors,
Replacing them with thoughts and acts of love,
Renewing our faith, our minds, and our bodies,
Reviving life within and around us,
Realizing that there is good within us,
Growing in our ability to feel and express that good,
Renovating our broken dreams and broken hearts,
Increasing our ability to own our light,
Reaching out to lovingly share that light with others.

— Donna Newman

There may be days when you get up in the morning
and things aren't the way you had hoped they would be.
That's when you have to tell yourself that things will get better.
There are times when people disappoint you and let you down,
but those are the times when you must remind yourself
to trust your own judgments and opinions,
to keep your life focused on believing in yourself
    and all that you are capable of.

There will be challenges to face
and changes to make in your life,
and it is up to you to accept them.
Constantly keep yourself headed in the right direction for you.
It may not be easy at times, but in those times of struggle
you will find a stronger sense of who you are,
and you will also see yourself developing
into the person you have always wanted to be.

Life is a journey through time, filled with many choices;
each of us will experience life in our own special way.
So when the days come that are filled
with frustration and unexpected responsibilities,
remember to believe in yourself
and all you want your life to be,
because the challenges and changes will only
help you to find the dreams
that you know are meant to come true for you.

— Deanna Beisser

ACCEPTANCE

Acceptance means that you
   can find the serenity within
to let go of the past
   with its mistakes and regrets,
move into the future
   with a new perspective,
and appreciate the opportunity
   to take a second chance.

Acceptance means you'll find security again
when difficult times come into your life,
and comfort to relieve any pain.
You'll find new dreams, fresh hopes,
   and forgiveness of the heart.

Acceptance does not mean that
   you will always be perfect.
It simply means that
   you'll always overcome imperfection.

Acceptance is the road to peace —
   letting go of the worst,
holding on to the best,
   and finding the hope inside
that continues throughout life.

Acceptance is the heart's best defense,
love's greatest asset, and the easiest way
   to keep believing in yourself and others.

— Regina Hill

Accept what comes to you
totally and completely so that you
can appreciate it, learn from it, and
then let it go.

— Deepak Chopra

Sometimes when we pray for miracles, what
we're really praying for is help in skipping steps, for
shortcuts. The simple act of acceptance, of returning
to each step of our path, can often bring us the
miracle we need. Then we see the truth. The real
miracle is one always available to each of us: it's the
miracle of acceptance. We can go where we want to
go, one step at a time.

— Melody Beattie

Anyone can carry his burden, however hard,
    until nightfall.
Anyone can do his work, however hard,
    for one day.

— Robert Louis Stevenson

After a While

After a while you learn
the subtle difference between
holding a hand and chaining a soul
and you learn
that love doesn't mean leaning
and company doesn't always mean security.
And you begin to learn
that kisses aren't contracts
and presents aren't promises
and you begin to accept your defeats
with your head up and your eyes ahead
with the grace of a woman, not the grief of a child
and you learn
to build all your roads on today
because tomorrow's ground is too uncertain for plans
and futures have a way of falling down in mid-flight.
After a while you learn
that even sunshine burns
if you get too much
so you plant your own garden
and decorate your own soul
instead of waiting for someone to bring you flowers.
And you learn that you really can endure
you really are strong
you really do have worth
and you learn
and you learn
with every goodbye, you learn.

— Veronica A. Shoffstall

Life is difficult. Think of breaking up the difficulties into small pieces, small steps. And share the difficulties — then they may become bearable. The secret is learning to live with and to use the difficulties one encounters.

— Bernie S. Siegel, M.D.

Remember how a walking trip always seems shorter if we concentrate, not on the total distance to our destination, but just the distance to the next milepost. In the same way, we should concentrate on living within today. Then better tomorrows will inevitably follow.

— Dale Carnegie

Never look down to test the ground before taking your next step: only he who keeps his eye fixed on the far horizon will find his right road.

— Dag Hammarskjöld

You'll Get Through This...
One Day at a Time

Try not to worry. Try to look at what you're going through as a challenge rather than an obstacle, a time to develop patience. To achieve more objectivity, detach yourself from the struggle. Have confidence in yourself, and realize that you can change your attitude even if you can't change the circumstances.

Look closely at your troubles. Don't let them cause you to give up. Befriend them and learn from them. Feel them lose their power over you. Allow them to teach you what you want to know and move on. Try not to be afraid.

You're a survivor. You're going to handle this. You're going to find strength you didn't know you had and grace to deal with whatever comes along. Pretty soon, you'll be on the other side, and it's just a matter of time until you will look back on this time in your life and draw strength from the knowledge that even though the road was rocky, you persevered and carried on.

— Donna Fargo

Resolve to be thyself: and know, that he who finds himself, loses his misery.

— Matthew Arnold

We bring about new beginnings by deciding to bring about endings. To renew your life you must be willing to change, to make an effort to leave behind the things that compromise your wholeness. The universe rushes to support you whenever you attempt to take a step forward. Any time you seek to be in harmony with life, to make yourself feel more whole, all the blessings that flow from God stream toward you, to bolster you and encourage you, because all life is biased on the side of supporting itself.

— Susan L. Taylor

Remember this, and also be persuaded of its truth — the future is not in the hands of fate, but in ourselves.

— Jules Jusserand

It matters not what you are thought to be, but what you are.

— Syrus

Every day is a birthday, for every day we are born anew.

— Ellen Browning Scripps

An essential part of the process of healing has to do with going into the shadow aspects of ourselves — the aspects that, out of fear, we have denied, disowned, or suppressed. Beginning in a gradual, safe, and comfortable way, we can accept and include them. Then, by allowing them their natural expression, we start to become more fully integrated human beings.

— Shakti Gawain

The tree which needs two arms to span its girth sprang from the tiniest shoot. Yon tower, nine stories high, rose from a little mound of earth. A journey of a thousand miles began with a single step.

— Lao-tse

The man who removes a mountain begins by carrying away small stones.

— Chinese Proverb

Many people
go from one thing
to another
searching for happiness
But with each new venture
they find themselves
more confused
and less happy
until they discover
that what they are
searching for
is inside themselves
and what will make them happy
is sharing their real selves
with the ones they love

— Susan Polis Schutz

Above the cloud
with its shadow
Is the star
with its light.

— Victor Hugo

Put knowledge, faith, and ideals into action...

Create an ideal for your life that you are willing to follow. Let it be something that is creative and constructive, never destructive or for the self alone. Identify for yourself what higher force you really believe in. Then act as if you have faith in that higher force that you will be guided and shown the way through your life, as well as through your search for healing. In other words, act as if these things are real in your life, and then <u>take action</u>.

— William A. McGarey, M.D.

The little troubles and worries of life, so many of which we meet, may be as stumbling blocks in our way, or we may make them steppingstones to a noble character and to Heaven.

Troubles are often the tools by which God fashions us for better things.

— Henry Ward Beecher

A whole person is one who has both walked with God and wrestled with the devil.

— Carl G. Jung

Lord, make me an instrument
   of your peace.
Where there is hatred,
   let me sow love;
where there is injury, pardon;
where there is doubt, faith;
where there is despair, hope;
where there is darkness, light;
and where there is sadness, joy.

— St. Francis of Assisi

God grant me the strength
to reach out for my dreams
and see the world
with understanding and love,
and to believe in the beauty
of life and the dignity of mankind.

— Andrew Harding Allen

If you have occasional spells of despondency and self-pity, if once in a while you begin to feel sorry for yourself, don't despair! The sun has a sinking spell every night, but it rises again all right the next morning.

— Richard C. Hertz

One thing that comes out in myths is that at the bottom of the abyss comes the voice of salvation. The black moment is the moment when the real message of transformation is going to come. At the darkest moment comes the light.

— Joseph Campbell

Keep in mind at all times
that you are very capable
of dealing with any complications
that life has to offer
So
do whatever you must
feel whatever you must
and keep in mind at all times
that we all
grow wiser and
become more sensitive and
are able to enjoy life more
after we go through
hard times

— Susan Polis Schutz

Though nothing can
bring back the hour of
Splendour in the grass,
of glory in the flower;
we will grieve not,
rather find strength in
what remains behind.

— William Wordsworth

We create our reality with our minds. If we want to change our reality, then it's time for us to change our minds. We do this by choosing to think and speak in new and positive ways. I learned a long time ago that if I would change my thinking, I could change my life. Changing our thinking is really dropping our limitations. As we drop our limitations, we begin to be aware of the infinity of life all around us. We begin to understand that we are already perfect, whole, and complete. Each day gets easier.

— Louise L. Hay

Recovery from any illness involves the body, the mind, and the spirit. Together, these three elements make up who we are, and true healing includes all these aspects of the self. Like a three-legged stool, recovery cannot stay upright and balanced unless all three "legs" are equally strong.

— Joseph D. Beasley
and Susan Knightly

In every event, in every circumstance, we have a choice of perspective. Faced with difficulty, we can choose between disappointment and curiosity as our mind-set. The choice is ours. Will we focus on what we see as lacking or will we look for the new good that is emerging? In every moment, however perilous or sorrowful it may feel, there is the seed of our greater happiness, greater expansion, and greater abundance.

— Julia Cameron

Now is the only time over which we have dominion.

— Leo Tolstoy

What you are, so is your world.

— James L. Allen

The only conquests which are permanent, and leave no regrets, are our conquests over ourselves.

— Napoleon Bonaparte

What to Do When You're Feeling a Little Overwhelmed by It All...

Some days are better than others.
Some are a little bit worse.
Sometimes everything works out okay.
Sometimes you can't get past the hurts.

When things get a little too stressful and you wonder how you'll make it through, you need to take everything a day at a time, and do what works <u>for you</u>.

Find a place in your heart where you see the way through to the truths about how things can be. Use your inner strength and your quiet resolve and all your positive qualities. Know that you're in the prayers of others. Whisper a few of your own. You don't have to do it all by yourself. Rest assured that you're never alone.

You're a strong and special person.
The very best is wished for you.
Have faith that tomorrow will bring brighter days.
And always have faith in... you.

— Marin McKay

Survivors Always Find a Way to Make the Best of Life

Survivors are people who have faced adversity and won. They've had all the odds against them, yet they've found a way to reach their goals.

Survivors are people who have been hurt by circumstances, by others, or just by being in the wrong place at the wrong time — but they don't allow themselves to live in pain forever. They go on, because they're brave enough and strong enough to overcome. They face the future with purpose, for they believe that time is on their side and each effort will pay off.

Survivors know how to make the best of life. They have an optimistic attitude and a winning spirit. That's how they reach their goals and why success is now the story of their lives.

— Barbara J. Hall

We cannot change the past;
we just need to keep
    the good memories
and acquire wisdom
from the mistakes we've made.
We cannot predict the future;
we just need to hope and pray
for the best and what is right,
and believe that's how it will be.
We can live a day at a time,
enjoying the present
and always seeking to become
a more loving and better person.

— Karen Berry

You better live your best and
act your best and think your
best today; for today is the
sure preparation for tomorrow
and all the other tomorrows
that follow.

— Harriet Martineau

It doesn't matter your age, or your color,
or whether your parents
loved you or not
(Maybe they wanted to, but couldn't.)
Let that go.
It belongs to the past.
You belong to the NOW.

It doesn't matter what you have been.
The wrong you may have done.
The mistakes you've made.
The people you've hurt.

You are forgiven.
You are accepted.
You are okay.
You are loved — in spite of everything.
So love yourself, and nourish the seed within you.

Celebrate you.
Begin NOW.
Start anew.
Give yourself a new birth today...
Today can be a new beginning, a new thing, a new life!

— Clyde Reid

WHAT TOMORROW'S FOR...

The reason for tomorrow
is to help to make sense of today.
Tomorrow is a brand-new chance
to begin a brand-new day.

The things that seem so difficult today,
and the problems that seem so high,
will be easier to handle if you understand
that things will get better by and by.

The purpose of tomorrow is to take
what we've learned from the past
and turn it into serenity
and happiness that lasts.

Your mountains will be so much easier
to climb in the light of a brand-new day.
With the passage of time, you'll often find
new strength and new pathways.

That is what tomorrow's for...
for hopes and dreams come true.
May every tomorrow be a beautiful day...
especially for you.

— Alin Austin

Each dawn is the
beginning of a
new life
Live life day by day
to understand
the joy that is
in your heart

— Louise Bradford Lowell

A man should never be ashamed to say he
has been in the wrong, which is but saying
in other words that he is wiser today than
he was yesterday.

— Alexander Pope

I believe that if
things don't turn
out the way I want
them to,
it's because there's
a better way
up ahead.

— Anonymous

WHAT IS HEALING?

———————✢———————

Healing is natural. It's not magical; it's not mystical. It doesn't require some esoteric intervention. It's your birthright, and mine. Everybody has the capacity for healing. We do it with each other all the time and we don't even know it.

Healing is the very ground of being. Everything is moving toward wholeness. And that's all healing is, that movement. Our task is not to make something happen but to uncover what is already happening in us and in others, and to recognize and foster those conditions that nurture it. That's all.

We can do that with ritual or prayer, or with many different approaches and techniques. We can simply sit and be together and think about our true nature. No one technique is inherently any better than another. It's simply a matter of learning to trust the natural healing process in all of us and moving freely with it.

— Rachel Naomi Remen

To me, healing is releasing from the past. It is retraining my mind so as not to see the shadow of the past on anyone. It is learning not to make interpretations of people's behavior or motives. It is letting go of the desire to want to change another person. It is letting go of expectations, assumptions, and the desire to control or manipulate another person....

Healing is knowing that forgiveness is the key to happiness and offers me everything that I want. Healing is knowing that the only reality in the universe is love, and that love is the most important healer known to the world.

To heal is to trust in a creative force that is loving and forgiving, and to know in our hearts that there is no separation and we are all joined in love with God and each other. It means that all hearts and minds are joined as one....

Healing is letting go of the fearful child so many of us carry inside, and awakening to the innocent child who has always been within us.

— Gerald Jampolsky

My Wounded Child

Years ago the child in me was wounded by the world,
well meaning as it was.
The scars of yesterday remain etched on my being,
taking their toll on all my days and nights.
Looking back, I can see the errors of those around me.
Little did they know the pain and suffering
they would bring me.
Now that I am older I search for that loving open child
that was.
But he remains in hiding from the pain that today might bring.
I want to set him free,
so that my life can be anew. But to reach him I must look
deep into the pain and the past. He protects himself with
games that he plays. Games of guilt and anger and fear and
resentment.
There is no winner in these games. For me to be free he must
be free to act and react not as the world expects
but as he feels is right.
Those around may not understand the turmoil and grief I feel for
his suffering. I'm not even sure who he is anymore but I know when he
comes forth that I will love him.
For he is the me I used to be and want to be again.
The me that is real.
I have missed him all these years and it is time for him to have his say.
To guide my feelings and my growth. It is time for him to set my world
right. He has been gone too long.
I welcome him now to brighten my future and change my ways.
To help me laugh and love again in ways only he knows how.
For when he returns, you may not know me. But that's ok,
for he will love you just the same. He will bring a smile to your
face and love to your heart.

— Tim Connor

Life

I feel I'm on a roller coaster,
Especially these past few weeks.
One day I'm up, the next I'm down,
When balance is what I seek.

On one day I deal with the present,
Or the past I'm working through;
And then come my fears for the future,
Uncertainties old and new....

But also mixed in with the hard times
Are the small moments of joy.
Times I am blessed with hope and with peace
And friends whom I enjoy.

Life is comprised of both good and bad
No matter what I go through.
Moments of laughter and joy and love,
Mixed with the old and the new.

— Wendy Apgar

Every mountain means at least two valleys.

— Anonymous

Do Not Be Afraid...

The greater the obstacle the
more glory in overcoming it.

— Molière

Healing is peeling away the barriers
of fear that keep us unaware of our
true nature of love, peace, and rich
interconnection with the web of life.
Healing is the rediscovery of who we
are and who we have always been.

— Joan Borysenko

Probably he who never made a
mistake never made a discovery.

— Samuel Smiles

Fear knocked at the door. Faith
answered. No one was there.

— Old English Legend

It is only by going down into the abyss
that we recover the treasures of life.
Where you stumble,
there lies your treasure.
The very cave you are afraid to enter
turns out to be the source of
what you were looking for.

— Joseph Campbell

In the midst of winter, I finally
learned that there was in me
an invincible summer.

— Albert Camus

The nicest thing about the future is that it
comes one day at a time.

— Anonymous

Be True to Yourself, No Matter What Anyone Else May Think

Right now, you
are struggling with your inner world.
You are asking yourself
    how you feel about everything
and if you are really happy.
You are changing into
    the exact person
that you were hoping to become,
but now you find that these changes
    are causing difficulties
for the people around you.
They want you to remain
    the same person that you've been;
they may even want you to be
    something for them
rather than being yourself.
But now is the time to make
    a statement about your life.
You must continue to follow
    your own chosen path
and make alterations in
    your lifestyle.

You will find your new place
in the circle of your loved ones,
but keep in mind that
everyone must create their own
sense of self and happiness.
No one should be shaped or confined
by someone else's ideals of
what they should be.
Strive for your own beliefs
and desires;
continue to make your world complete
by being yourself.
Every day, discover something
new and unique about yourself,
and remember that happiness
and contentment in life
come when you focus on
your own dreams,
being yourself, and enjoying
every minute of your life.

— Dena Dilaconi

FIND A PLACE
OF SERENITY...

Find places of healing. Discover people, things, and places that nourish your soul, bring you back to center, help you heal.

Life is not an endurance contest. Not anymore. We are not in a race to see how long we can go without, how much we can go without, how much pain we can stay in. Although sometimes we go through dry spells and droughts, we are not cactuses.

There is a place in each of us that wants to heal, that can heal, that will heal. It's a peaceful place, one of nourishment, replenishment, peace, safety, comfort, and joy. It's a place of love and acceptance. It's a place of forgiveness, honesty, openness, nurturing, and kindness. You can find it quickly, if that's what you're seeking. You will recognize it instantly because of how it feels. It will bring you back to center. It will bring you back to calm. It will bring you back to joy.

— Melody Beattie

Let your task be to render yourself
worthy of love and this even more for your
own happiness than for that of another.

— Maurice Maeterlinck

It is in your power to withdraw into yourself whenever
you desire. Perfect tranquility within consists in the good
ordering of the mind, — the realm of your own.

— Marcus Aurelius

If you seek peace and love first, if you learn to
become mindfully present, you'll find that good things
seem to be attracted to you without your even having
to specify them. When you think about using the power
of your mind in daily life, remember that peace is the
most important goal, because thoughts of peace open
the heart to love, and they close the mind to fear. Peace
and love are the frame of reference through which we
discover the mind's true power.

— Joan and Miroslav Borysenko

Nothing wastes more energy than worrying.
The longer one carries a problem, the heavier it gets.
Don't take things too seriously.
Live a life of serenity, not a life of regrets.

— Douglas Pagels

Trust the Process of Life

If something happens that you feel you have no control over, then affirm a positive statement immediately. Keep saying it over and over to yourself until you move through that little space. When things don't feel right, you might say this to yourself: "All is well, all is well, all is well." Whenever you feel the urge to control things, you could say, "I trust the process of life."... In this way, whatever happens is okay because you are in harmony with the flow of life.

— Louise L. Hay

Remember: the will is mighty. The steadfast decision and concerted effort to get better will begin to empower you. Hold fast to your desires and positive affirmation for wholeness and believe that you will recover completely. Don't be afraid to ask God for help, and it's important to thank Him and trust in Him that your prayers will be answered. He delights in our trust and praise and faithfulness.

— Donna Fargo

A Daily Affirmation, a Lifetime Inspiration

A hill is not too hard to climb,
Taken one step at a time.
One step is not too much to take,
One try is not too much to make.

One step, one try, one song, one smile
Will shortly stretch into a mile.
And everything worthwhile was done
By small steps taken one by one.

To reach the goal you started for,
Take one step more...
take one step more.

— J. D. Freeman

Keep the Faith

Sometimes, the road to recovery is a long one. There are detours filled with disappointments and frustrations. It is difficult to move ahead, not knowing what the future may bring.

You are on that road now, and all the medicine in the world cannot reassure you. You hold life by the reins, afraid they'll slip. Right now, the pain around you limits your vision and growth.

We all take life for granted. And when the hardships come, we feel that we are being tested — sometimes beyond the point of endurance.

But take heart and keep the faith. Know that at the end of the dark tunnel there is a light. The answer lies within you, in the spirit with which you brave the battle. The pain and suffering are not you, but only a part of you.

Hold your head up, and keep true to the brightness within yourself. Move on and never look back, filled with hope and love for what you have endured. And reach out with warm hands and an open heart to help others like you — who can learn to move on, too.

— Josie Willis

...And Remember This...

How you live today
affects all your tomorrows.
Remember that turning down
the wrong road
is part of the journey,
and finding the way back
is your challenge.
Remember that if you keep God
close to your heart,
home will never be far away.
There will be expectations not met,
promises lost, tears,
and moments of despair.
Remember, however,
to be grateful for the sunshine
and to find hope in the rainbow.
Remember to laugh from your soul
and always hold on to your dreams.

— Bernadette Garzarelli

WITHIN YOU, THERE IS A SEED OF COURAGE

There is a seed in the
heart of everyone
that lies quietly at the bottom
of the soul.
This seed sleeps patiently,
waiting for the chance to grow
and survive against all
that will attempt to
choke it out.
It is not visible to everyone;
its presence is not even always known.
But suddenly, someday,
when the need arises —
a hole will be torn in the soul,
the sun will shine through...
and your courage will be born.

— Christine Peterson

Whether you be man or woman you
will never do anything in this world
without courage. It is the greatest
quality of the mind next to honor.

— James L. Allen

Courage is resistance to fear, mastery of fear —
not absence of fear.

— Mark Twain

They can conquer who believe they can.

— Virgil

NEVER GIVE UP HOPE

Hope is a beautiful answer to many difficult questions. Hope only asks that you believe. Hope only wants you to receive. Hope is "hanging in there" until help arrives. Whenever a day didn't go as planned, hope is there as a comforting guide to help you understand.

Hope is a quiet, personal place where you can always take shelter. Hope is the warm and welcomed knowledge that beautiful possibilities exist. Hope is all these special things, and in simply knowing this —

When hope is all you've got...
    you still have got a lot.

            — Collin McCarty

Be like the bird
That, pausing in her flight
Awhile on boughs too slight,
    Feels them give way
Beneath her and yet sings,
Knowing that she hath wings.

            — Victor Hugo

Strong hope is a much greater stimulant of life than any single realized joy could be.

            — Friedrich Nietzsche

There is no medicine like hope,
no incentive so great, and no
tonic so powerful as expectation
of something better tomorrow.

— Orison Swett Marden

Hope is the thing with feathers
That perches in the soul,
And sings the tune without the words,
And never stops at all.

— Emily Dickinson

Hope is the better half of courage.

— Honoré de Balzac

Hope is life and life is hope.

— Adele Shreve

LETTING GO...

To have a hold on us... misery must be mentally reentered daily, and the doorway we provide is our preoccupation with what happened. There is very little that can hurt you once you learn how to release your mind from what you have unconsciously picked up during the day.

— Hugh Prather

However you have used gone days, you can start afresh each morning, if you so desire. You can use this day for consolidating past gains of spirit, brain and hand, or you can use it for tearing down the old structure of self and laying the foundations for a new building. Each night of life is a wall between today and the past. Each morning is the open door to a new world — new vistas, new aims, new tryings....

However discouraging your days may have been thus far, keep this thought burning brightly in your mind — Life Begins Each Morning!

— Leigh Mitchell Hodges

*W*hen things are not going right
don't give up — just try harder
Give yourself freedom to try out new things
Laugh and have a good time
Open yourself up to love
Take part in the beauty of nature
Be appreciative of all that you have
Help those less fortunate than you
Work towards peace in the world
Live life to the fullest
Create your own dreams and
follow them until they are a reality

— Susan Polis Schutz

*I*f you can forgive yourself as well as others
and learn from your mistakes,
problems and heartaches will be steppingstones
on your path to growing wiser and stronger.

If you can love yourself as well as others,
you will learn acceptance and understanding.

If you believe you are unique and wonderful,
then you will learn to change what you can,
make a difference when you can,
and accept the things
you can't do anything about.

— Barbara Cage

WHEN SOMEONE YOU CARE ABOUT IS IN RECOVERY...

⸙

When someone you love has difficulties, listen. When you're feeling terrible that you can't provide a cure, listen. When you don't know what to offer the people you care about, listen, listen, listen.

— Bernie S. Siegel, M.D.

The use of love is to heal.
When it flows without effort
from the depth of the self,
love creates health.

— Deepak Chopra

Love

There is no difficulty that enough love will not conquer; No disease that enough love will not heal; No door that enough love will not open; No gulf that enough love will not bridge; No wall that enough love will not throw down; No sin that enough love will not redeem...

It makes no difference how deeply seated may be the trouble; How hopeless the outlook; How muddled the tangle; How great the mistake. A sufficient realization of love will dissolve it all... If only you could love enough you would be the happiest and most powerful being in the world.

— Emmet Fox

Easy Does It...

*F*inish every day and be done with it.... You have done what you could; some blunders and absurdities no doubt crept in; forget them as soon as you can. Tomorrow is a new day; you shall begin it well and serenely, and with too high a spirit to be cumbered with your old nonsense. This day is all that is good and fair. It is too dear, with its hopes and invitations, to waste a moment on... yesterdays.

— Ralph Waldo Emerson

*G*o confidently in the direction of your dreams! Live the life you've imagined! As you simplify your life, the laws of the universe will be simpler, solitude will not be solitude, poverty will not be poverty, nor weakness, weakness.

— Henry David Thoreau

*S*implicity is an exact medium between too little and too much.

— Sir Joshua Reynolds

Learn to say no...

The most important thing you can do for yourself in a crisis situation is to learn to manage your time. You have to put yourself first on your agenda. The best way to do that is to learn to say no. You can no longer afford to live within the perception that you're going to miss out on something potentially life-changing if you're not there, whether the event is a new movie that everyone's going to see, or a family wedding, or a business meeting.

— Caroline Myss

God, give us grace to accept with
SERENITY
the things that cannot be changed,
COURAGE
to change the things which should be changed, and the
WISDOM
to distinguish the one from the other.

— Reinhold Niebuhr

ACCEPTING THE HELP OF OTHERS...

As human beings, we're not perfect,
and we're not supposed to be.
But that's not always an easy thing
    for us to realize.
The best we can do is to do the
    best we can,
give it our all, and always give thanks.
We don't make it alone in this world.
We're lucky that there are people
placed in our path to guide us,
protect us, and touch our lives
so that we can get through it all...
one day at a time.

— Julia Escobar

We are all travellers in the
wilderness of this world,
and the best that we find
    in our travels
is an honest friend.

— Robert Louis Stevenson

The priceless gifts we give to each other
are not the ones wrapped
in fancy paper,
but the gifts we give when
we give of ourselves.
It is the love that we share.
It is the comfort we lend in times of need.
It is the moments we spend together
helping each other follow our dreams.
The most priceless gifts we can give
are the understanding and caring
that come from the heart.
And each and every one of us
has these gifts to offer...
through the gift of ourselves.

— Ben Daniels

We are here
to help
each other.

— Polar Eskimo Saying

You Can Do It!

Hang in there and have patience
with yourself and the situation.
Live in the moment, one day at a time,
not fretting about the past
    or worrying about the future.
You have strength enough for the present,
and that is all you need for now.
Allow yourself the luxury of peace,
and don't take on more than you have to.
Learn to let go.
Refuse negative thoughts;
replace them with positive ones.
Look for the good things in your life
and make a point to appreciate them.
Believe in yourself and know
    that you have the power.
You are ultimately the one
    in charge of your life,
and the only person in the world
    who can change it.
No matter how much others
    are pulling for you
or how much anyone else cares,
you must do what needs to be done
to make your present and future
everything you want and need it to be.
You can do it!

— Barbara Cage

The road to recovery
is sometimes slow.
But may your path
be made easier
just by knowing
that God is watching over you
while friends and family
stand beside you,
caring and concerned.
Together,
they all join forces for you,
praying that your recovery
will be complete and full
and soon.

— Linda E. Knight

Know that in the grand scheme of things, we live in a world where rainy days eventually give way to sunnier skies, and where simply believing in tomorrow takes you halfway up the mountain to getting beyond any difficulties.

May you have the companionship of comfort on every path you take and the gentleness of peace. May you find serenity and strength and every single thing… that will put your heart at ease.

— R. L. Keith

Walk Your Path
One Step at a Time

Life's circumstances are not always what you might wish them to be. The pattern of life does not necessarily go as you plan. Beyond any understanding, you may at times be led in different directions that you never imagined, dreamed, or designed. Yet if you had never put any effort into choosing a path, or tried to carry out your dream, then perhaps you would have no direction at all.

Rather than wondering about or questioning the direction your life has taken, accept the fact that there is a path before you now. Shake off the "why's" and "what if's," and rid yourself of confusion. Whatever was — is in the past. Whatever is — is what's important. The past is a brief reflection. The future is yet to be realized. Today is here.

Walk your path one step at a time — with courage, faith, and determination. Keep your head up, and cast your dreams to the stars. Soon your steps will become firm and your footing will be solid again. A path that you never imagined will become the most comfortable direction you could have ever hoped to follow.

Keep your belief in yourself and walk into your new journey. You will find it magnificent, spectacular, and beyond your wildest imaginings.

— Vicki Silvers

ACKNOWLEDGMENTS

We gratefully acknowledge the permission granted by the following authors, publishers, and authors' representatives to reprint poems or excerpts from their publications.

Foundation for A Course in Miracles® for "Every situation..." from A COURSE IN MIRACLES®. Copyright © 1975, 1992, 1999 by the Foundation for A Course in Miracles. All rights reserved. Reprinted by permission of the Foundation for A Course in Miracles®, 1275 Tennanah Lake Road, Roscoe, NY 12776-5905.

Harmony Books, a division of Random House, Inc., for "Accept what comes..." and "The use of love..." from JOURNEY INTO HEALING by Deepak Chopra, M.D. Copyright © 1994 by Deepak Chopra, M.D. All rights reserved. Reprinted by permission.

Crown Publishers, Inc., a division of Random House, Inc., for "Learn to say no..." from WHY PEOPLE DON'T HEAL AND HOW THEY CAN by Caroline Myss, Ph.D. Copyright © 1997 by Caroline Myss. And for "Recovery from any illness..." from FOOD FOR RECOVERY by Joseph D. Beasley, M.D. and Susan Knightly. Copyright © 1994 by Joseph D. Beasley, M.D. and Susan Knightly. All rights reserved. Reprinted by permission.

HarperCollins Publishers, Inc. for "Sometimes when we pray..." and "Find places of healing..." from JOURNEY TO THE HEART: DAILY MEDITATIONS ON THE PATH TO FREEING YOUR SOUL by Melody Beattie. Copyright © 1996 by Melody Beattie. For "Life is difficult..." and "When someone you love..." from HOW TO LIVE BETWEEN OFFICE VISITS: A GUIDE TO LIFE, LOVE AND HEALTH by Bernie S. Siegel, M.D. Copyright © 1993 by Bernie S. Siegel. And for "It doesn't matter..." from CELEBRATE THE TEMPORARY by Clyde Reid. Copyright © 1972 by Clyde Reid. All rights reserved. Reprinted by permission.

Veronica A. Shoffstall for "After a While." Copyright © 1971 by Veronica A. Shoffstall. All rights reserved. Reprinted by permission.

PrimaDonna Entertainment Corp. for "You'll Get Through This... One Day at a Time" and "Remember: the will is mighty..." by Donna Fargo. Copyright © 1999 by PrimaDonna Entertainment Corp. All rights reserved. Reprinted by permission.

Essence Communications, Inc. for "We bring about new beginnings..." from IN THE SPIRIT: THE INSPIRATIONAL WRITINGS OF SUSAN L. TAYLOR, published by Amistad. Copyright © 1993 by Essence Communications, Inc. All rights reserved. Reprinted by permission.

Jeremy P. Tarcher, a division of Penguin Putnam, Inc., for "An essential part..." by Shakti Gawain, "Healing is peeling away the barriers..." by Joan Borysenko, "Healing is natural..." by Rachel Naomi Remen, and "To me, healing is releasing..." by Gerald Jampolsky from HEALERS ON HEALING edited by Benjamin Shield and Richard Carlson. Copyright © 1989 by Benjamin Shield and Richard Carlson. And for "In every event..." from BLESSINGS: PRAYERS AND DECLARATIONS FOR A HEARTFUL LIFE by Julia Cameron. Copyright © 1998 by Julia Cameron. All rights reserved. Reprinted by permission.

Putnam Berkley, a division of Penguin Putnam, Inc., for "Put knowledge, faith, and ideals into action..." from IN SEARCH OF HEALING by William A. McGarey, M.D. Copyright © 1996 by William A. McGarey, M.D. All rights reserved. Reprinted by permission.

Hay House, Inc. for "We create our reality..." and "Trust the Process of Life" from MEDITATIONS TO HEAL YOUR LIFE by Louise L. Hay. Copyright © 1994 by Louise L. Hay. And for "If you seek peace..." from THE POWER OF THE MIND TO HEAL by Joan Borysenko, Ph.D. and Miroslav Borysenko, Ph.D. Copyright © 1994 by Joan Borysenko and Miroslav Borysenko. All rights reserved. Reprinted by permission of Hay House, Inc. Carlsbad, CA.

Josie Willis for "On Your Road to Recovery...." Copyright © 1999 by Josie Willis. All rights reserved. Reprinted by permission.

Tim Connor for "My Wounded Child." Copyright © 1999 by Tim Connor. All rights reserved. Reprinted by permission.

Wendy Apgar for "Life." Copyright © 1997 by Wendy Apgar. All rights reserved. Reprinted by permission.

Barbara J. Hall for "Survivors Always Find a Way to Make the Best of Life." Copyright © 1999 by Barbara J. Hall. All rights reserved. Reprinted by permission.

Christine Peterson for "Within You, There Is a Seed of Courage." Copyright © 2000 by Christine Peterson. All rights reserved. Reprinted by permission.

Barbara Cage for "You Can Do It!" Copyright © 2000 by Barbara Cage. All rights reserved. Reprinted by permission.

Doubleday, a division of Random House, Inc., for "To have a hold on us..." from NOTES ON HOW TO LIVE IN THE WORLD... AND STILL BE HAPPY by Hugh Prather. Copyright © 1986 by Hugh Prather. All rights reserved. Reprinted by permission.

A careful effort has been made to trace the ownership of poems used in this anthology in order to obtain permission to reprint copyrighted materials and give proper credit to the copyright owners. If any error or omission has occurred, it is completely inadvertent, and we would like to make corrections in future editions provided that written notification is made to the publisher:

SPS STUDIOS, INC., P.O. Box 4549, Boulder, Colorado 80306.